Mind Your Thoughts
By
Glenn Wolkoff

Be happy and you will have
everything you desire.

Mind Your Thoughts
By
Glenn Wolkoff

Vitae Mind Publishing
Glenn Wolkoff
4804 Laurel Canyon Blvd., #190
Valley Village, CA 91607
www.vitaemind.com

Dear Mankind:

Physical life comes and goes for the briefest of moments. Live it wisely.

Explore the unknown. Create things. Do not destroy.

Be yourself. Do not be like everybody else.

Enjoy life, not things. Have experiences.

Love and heal yourself and others.

Be happy. Fix what does not work.

Contribute to mankind and the Universe.

∞ Glenn

Introduction

The purpose of meditation is to quiet the mind. Meditation removes the clutter of thoughts from everyday life, and also helps you to get in touch with your higher consciousness. It does take practice, so do not become discouraged.

Set aside 45 minutes each evening before you go to sleep. Sit in a quiet room, in a comfortable and relaxed position wearing loose clothing.

Close your eyes and breathe deeply, in through your nose and out slowly through your mouth. With each breath in, clear your mind of all thoughts, and feel your body relax. Repeat this 9 times before beginning.

This book contains 81 thoughts for meditation. There are 9 sets of 9 thoughts. Start with Set One and allow 5 minutes of meditation for each thought.

After your initial warm up of 9 deep breaths, read the first thought of the first set. Close your eyes and continue your deep breathing as you reflect on the thought and what it may mean to you and your life. Think of nothing else. Repeat this with each thought until you complete Set One.

It will take you at least 9 evenings to get through all of the sets in the book. You may want to repeat a set over and over again before moving on to the next set. Eventually, you will have your favorite thoughts that you will want to dedicate your meditations on.

Most people enjoy thoughts of wisdom, but rarely take the time to internalize them enough to be life changing.

Practice mindfulness in life and create ripples that will forever change your life.

This is not an instructional book on the art of meditation.

Table of Meditations

SET ONE

You are Source.

You can perform miracles.

You are a
spiritual being
with a thinking
mind having
human
experiences
through a
physical body.

Your life is eternal.

You are not your body.

Accept who you
are.

There is nothing
you cannot do.

Feel the energy
force that exists
connecting all
mankind to one
another and to
the rest of the
physical universe.

*Energy is
everything.*

SET TWO

All thoughts are energy.

You are "thinking energy."

You think,
therefore,
you create.

Thought and
energy creates
reality.

You will
understand how
thought and
energy creates
reality, once you
acknowledge your
spiritual nature.

You can transform
matter, energy,
and even life
through conscious
thought.

You are the
creator of your
own reality.

Life is yours to create!

*You determine
your life by what
you think.*

SET THREE

You can only
create what you
accept.

To create reality,
be conscious of
your thoughts.

You can create the
Universe as you
wish it to be.

You can bring
form to matter
merely by
observing it.

When human
thought interacts
with energy, it
can alter form.

Human thought
from the observer
in you, is what
gives mass to
matter.

*The physical
dimension is the
result of
imagination.*

You are ideas
taking form.

You get exactly
what you want in
life.

SET FOUR

What you expect is what will be.

*You can heal
yourself and heal
others.*

Wellness is based on energy, light, and vibration.

Your state of well-being is directly attributable to the energy that flows through you.

The right
combination of
thought and
energy can
spontaneously
heal any illness in
living form.

The right combination of thought and energy can spontaneously materialize any non-living form.

Enhancing
vibrational states
allows you to
enter the
quantum field.

Philosophy becomes truth once you experience it.

*Everyone you meet
is a reflection of
you.*

SET FIVE

Time does not exist.

If you live by time,
you do not live.

Lose track of time.

Time is an event
occurring in the
present moment.

All events have consequences.

All events start a chain of next events.

Every event in
your life is the
effect of a previous
cause.

For an accident to
happen, one must
plan and
participate in the
events that lead
up to it.

The only
difference between
common acts and
miracles is how
often they occur.

SET SIX

*To see a miracle,
look in the mirror.*

Always look for the extraordinary within the ordinary.

The ends can never justify the means.

See what no one
else can see.

Hear what people
do not say.

Know what no one
else can know.

You already know
everything; you
just need to
remember.

Suffering or not
having is never
the path to your
spiritual self.

Get over things
and move on
quickly.

SET SEVEN

You have "free-will" which is the ability to choose; the ability to accept or not accept.

Your greatest
power is your
free will.

You need three
things in life to be
happy: love,
wisdom, and
compassion.

Share compassion
with those who
have neither love
nor wisdom.

Happiness is a
state of mind.

Choose it!

It is a choice.

Happiness is the absence of negative thought.

Karma is a collection of all of your choices, actions, and non-actions that when added together equal your current state of being.

You have life debts that can only be paid through learning your life lessons and evolving.

*Enable people to
reach their
greatest good.*

Use all of your talents.

SET EIGHT

Do what makes you come alive.

Find what
you do best.

Live a life of purpose.

Have a cause.

*Live each day to
the fullest.*

Keep it simple.

Laugh often.

Respect and love
yourself.

Respect and love
others.

SET NINE

Protect mankind
by being respectful
of one another.

Great things are
only accomplished
in the lightest of
heart.

Measure success by
how little you
need.

Judge not and be free to live.

The difference
between beauty
and ugliness is a
judgment.

If you want to walk on water, see it as solid rather than as liquid.

Yeshua ben Joseph was here to show us the relationship between mind and matter and to demonstrate there was life after death.

Source is energy.
Source is spirit.
You are energy.
You are spirit.
Source is you.
You are Source.

Your reality is a manifestation of your thought.